# The Sleigh in the Hay

By Cameron Macintosh

It will be Jay's big day
on Sunday.

Kate and Dad will paint
a sleigh for Jay.
Kate will add a braided rope.

They kept the sleigh in the shed.

"Let's hide the sleigh with hay," said Kate.

Kate and Dad had a break, then went back to the shed.

“The bulls are munching up the hay!” Kate yelled.

"I will get fresh hay bales,"
said Dad.

Kate led the bulls away.

But Jay was on his way!

Hide Jay's sleigh!
There is no more hay in here!

Kate gave Jay a pail of grain.

“Hey, Jay!” she said.
“Take this grain
to the baby hens!”

Jay went down the trail.

Back in the shed,
Kate looked in a box.

A pile of plain sacks
was inside.

"Let's use these to hide the sleigh," Kate called.

"Great!" said Dad. "You have a quick brain, Kate!"

They laid eighteen sacks
on the sleigh,
just as Jay came back.

"Let's go and play, Jay,"
said Kate.

All Jay could see was a pile
of plain sacks!

## CHECKING FOR MEANING

1. What does Kate plan to give Jay for his birthday? *(Literal)*
2. What happened to the hay that was covering the sleigh? *(Literal)*
3. Why did Kate ask Jay to feed the baby chicks? *(Inferential)*

## EXTENDING VOCABULARY

| | |
|---|---|
| **braided** | What does the word *braided* mean? What can you braid, besides rope? Why did Kate braid some rope for the sleigh? |
| **pail** | What is a pail? What is another word you know that has a similar meaning to *pail*? |
| **plain** | Why did the author call the sacks *plain*? What else can be plain? If the sacks were not plain, what might they look like? |

## MOVING BEYOND THE TEXT

1. Why do you think Kate was so keen to hide the sleigh from Jay? Why is it nice for a gift to be a surprise?

2. Have you ever made someone a gift, or has someone made you a gift? What was the gift?

3. Kate and Dad planned to fix up the sleigh. What might they decide to do next? What kinds of tools or supplies might they need?

4. On Kate's farm, the bulls eat hay and the chickens eat grain. What other types of food might farm animals eat?

## TIME TO WRITE

Write about something you would like to fix up or change. It can be something in your classroom, at your school, at home or in your neighbourhood.

# PRACTICE WORDS